ALTERNATOR
BOOKS™

WORLD WAR II
SPIES AND
SECRET AGENTS

Stuart A. Kallen

Lerner Publications ◆ Minneapolis

Content consultant: Eric Juhnke, Professor of History, Briar Cliff University

Lerner Publications Company
A division of Lerner Publishing Group, Inc.
241 First Avenue North
Minneapolis, MN 55401 USA

For reading levels and more information, look up this title at www.lernerbooks.com.

Main body text set in Aptifer Slab LT Pro Regular 11.5/18.
Typeface provided by Linotype AG.

Library of Congress Cataloging-in-Publication Data

Names: Kallen, Stuart A., 1955– author.
Title: World War II spies and secret agents / by Stuart A. Kallen.
Other titles: World War Two spies and secret agents
Description: Minneapolis : Lerner Publications, 2018. | Series: Heroes of World War II | Includes bibliographical references and index. | Audience: Grade: 4 to 6. | Audience: Age: 8 to 12.
Identifiers: LCCN 2017009638 (print) | LCCN 2017012093 (ebook) | ISBN 9781512498202 (eb pdf) | ISBN 9781512486421 (lb : alk. paper)
Subjects: LCSH: World War, 1939–1945—Secret service—Juvenile literature. | Espionage—History—20th century—Juvenile literature. | Spies—History—20th century—Juvenile literature. | Spies—Biography—Juvenile literature.
Classification: LCC D810.S7 (ebook) | LCC D810.S7 K257 2018 (print) | DDC 940.54/860922—dc23

LC record available at https://lccn.loc.gov/2017009638

Manufactured in the United States of America
1-43466-33206-6/13/2017

CONTENTS

INTRODUCTION
A DARING ADVENTURE

In January 1940, British secret agent Merlin Minshall, along with a small team, rented six **barges**. They loaded the boats with cement and wired them with **explosives**. The plan was to send the barges down the Danube River in Romania and then blow them up at the river's narrowest point, known as the Iron Gates. If the plan worked, the cement-filled sunken barges would be very hard to move. This would block the

Britain moves troops after
World War II begins in 1939.

Danube for months and stop ships carrying war supplies to Germany.

As the barges sailed down the Danube, Minshall followed close behind in a high-speed boat. But the mission was doomed. Romanian spies working at the port had tipped off the **Nazis**, and German soldiers had secretly drained each barge of half its fuel.

The barges slowed to a halt before reaching the Iron Gates. Nazi officials arrived and searched the barges. They found the explosives. The Nazis tried to arrest Minshall, but he made a quick escape in his boat under a hail of Nazi gunfire. After a two-hour high-speed chase, Minshall got away.

BATTLE BEHIND THE SCENES

In the late 1930s, World War II (1939–1945) was brewing in Europe. Nazi Germany had joined forces with Italy, Japan, and others to form the Axis powers. Great Britain, France, and others, together known as the Allied powers, opposed the Axis powers. World War II began on September 1, 1939, when the Nazi army invaded Poland. The Allied powers declared war on Germany. Eventually the United States also joined the Allies.

For years, military troops battled in trenches, in the air, and at sea. But away from the front lines, Minshall and many other Allied spies and secret agents waged war in secret. These agents faced constant danger during World War II. They broke Axis codes, stole battle

Europe in World War II

International border
Non-Europe lands

GREAT BRITAIN

NORTH
ATLANTIC
OCEAN

GERMANY

POLAND

Danube River

FRANCE

ROMANIA

SPAIN

ITALY

N

Miles
0   100   200   300
0   200   400
Kilometers

plans, and stopped weapon programs. Their names
were known to only a few, but with their help, the
Allies eventually defeated the Axis powers and won
the war.

CHAPTER 1
MUSICAL MISSION

In November 1940, a man and a woman boarded a train in France. The woman was dressed in expensive furs and fancy clothes. The man wore glasses and had a mustache. They were on their way to Portugal.

The woman was Josephine Baker. She was one of the biggest stars in the world. Baker had become famous for her dazzling dances and sizzling songs.

Josephine Baker performed in New York City before moving to Paris, France.

Germany invaded France in 1940, and German soldiers were stationed in France for several years. Many French citizens worked in secret to fight against German control.

Sometimes she performed with a golden-eyed leopard named Chiquita.

When the train reached Spain, Spanish police checked their passports. Baker said that she was on her way to a concert and that the man with her was her assistant. The police were amazed and excited to see Baker. Baker and the man went all the way to Portugal, and nobody noticed that he had a fake passport and that they were carrying fifty-two pieces of top-secret information. Nobody ever guessed that Baker was a spy.

This group of French citizens, known as Maquis, fought against German control.

BECOMING A SPY

Baker was born in Saint Louis, Missouri, in 1906. She rose to fame in Paris in 1925 at a time when black culture was being celebrated in France. After France fell to the Nazis, the head of the French military intelligence service, Jacques Abtey, asked Baker to work with him. Because Baker traveled often and knew important people, she would make a great spy. Because of her fame, she was also unlikely to be suspected. Baker pledged her support: "The people of Paris have given . . . me their hearts, and I have given them mine. I am ready, Captain, to give them my life."

When Baker traveled, she carried huge suitcases

and lots of sheet music. The sheet music also held secret messages gathered by those fighting against the Germans. These messages contained information about Nazi troop movements, written in invisible ink. She also pinned notes and photos of German army bases to the inside of her dress. She passed messages and information to other spies and officials, who used the information to plan strategies against the Nazis.

STEM HIGHLIGHT

Secret messages written in invisible ink played an important role during World War II. The ink was made with special chemicals such as iron sulfate and cobalt salts. The messages only appeared when exposed to another chemical, called a reagent. One popular reagent was iodine **vapor**. It turned all invisible inks brown. The vapor colored the paper's fibers where the wet ink had been applied. The letter on the right is the same document before and after the reagent had been applied. Throughout the war, scientists worked to create new inks that could not be detected by iodine vapor, heat, or light. Many people also worked hard to reveal the secret messages written by the enemy.

CHAPTER 2
A REAL-LIFE JAMES BOND

In 1939 British writer Ian Fleming became part of
the British Naval Intelligence Division. The British
knew that the German military had many better
technologies than the Allied forces did at the time.
Fleming also knew that German intelligence units had
special forces to gather information during an attack.

**Before the war,
Fleming worked as a
newspaper reporter
and a stockbroker.**

During the war, the German army developed new weapons known as V-weapons. The V-1 (*pictured*) was a flying bomb. The V-2 was a much more destructive rocket.

These forces were known as **commandos**. In 1942 Fleming suggested that the British should come up with its own commandos. The group became known as 30 AU (Assault Unit). Fleming and his men learned skills such as parachuting, handling explosives, and picking locks.

SECRET THIEVES

The mission of 30 AU was to learn about Nazi technology. German scientists were designing new kinds of rockets, torpedoes, and submarines. The Allies feared these deadly weapons would help the Nazis win the war. Fleming's team broke into Nazi offices and labs to steal military information and equipment.

In 1944 and 1945, Fleming's skilled team of thirty-nine agents completed many missions. During the D-day invasion of Normandy, France, Fleming's men gathered information about German submarines. In another mission, 30 AU stole thousands of pages of secret codes, scientific papers, and scientific diaries. They also captured ten German scientists and took

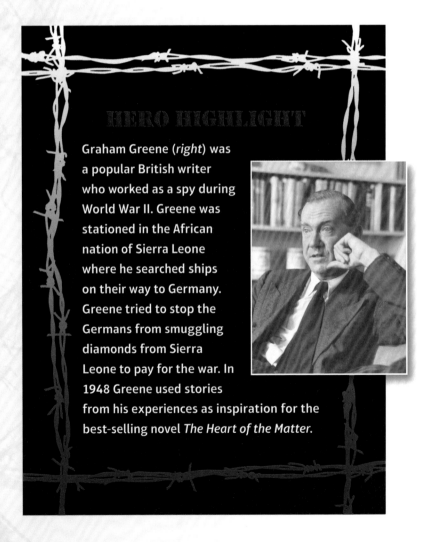

HERO HIGHLIGHT

Graham Greene (*right*) was a popular British writer who worked as a spy during World War II. Greene was stationed in the African nation of Sierra Leone where he searched ships on their way to Germany. Greene tried to stop the Germans from smuggling diamonds from Sierra Leone to pay for the war. In 1948 Greene used stories from his experiences as inspiration for the best-selling novel *The Heart of the Matter*.

James Bond continues to be a popular character. After twenty-four movies, the franchise shows no signs of slowing down.

them to Britain. Fleming's mission stopped the scientists from developing secret weapons such as superbombs and one-man submarines.

After the war ended, Fleming's secret missions inspired him to create the character James Bond. Bond was a secret agent known by the code name 007. Bond's exciting missions went on to be featured in thirty-six novels and twenty-four movies.

CHAPTER 3
THE LIMPING LADY

Posters all over France showed an illustration of a woman and had the warning: "The woman who limps is one of the most dangerous Allied agents in France. We must find and destroy her." The Nazis were determined to find and stop this woman, known as the Limping Lady, who was part of the French Resistance.

French Resistance fighters keep an eye on German soldiers in 1944.

Resistance fighters sabotaged railroads to make it more difficult for Germany to move troops and equipment.

It was March 1944, and French Resistance fighters were disrupting Nazi operations. The French Resistance was made up of women and men who worked in secret to fight the Nazis after Germany invaded France in June 1940. Each country Germany invaded had a Resistance. Resistance members conducted **guerrilla warfare**—they ambushed enemy soldiers and conducted raids against Nazi outposts. The Resistance also gathered information and passed it along to Allied leaders.

Meanwhile, an old woman with gray hair, who shuffled her feet when she walked and wore wide skirts, arrived in France. She moved around often and camped in barns and attics. She made sure members of the Resistance got supplies and reported on German troop movements. The Nazis never caught the Limping Lady. And they never suspected that this old woman was the Limping Lady in **disguise**.

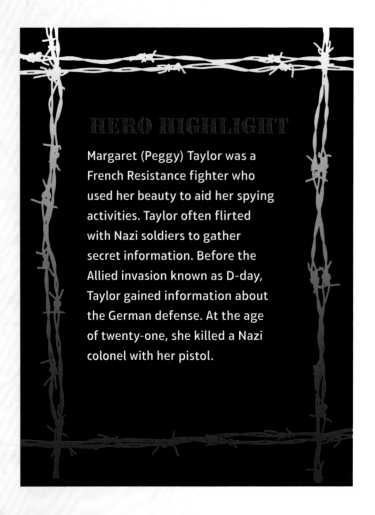

HERO HIGHLIGHT

Margaret (Peggy) Taylor was a French Resistance fighter who used her beauty to aid her spying activities. Taylor often flirted with Nazi soldiers to gather secret information. Before the Allied invasion known as D-day, Taylor gained information about the German defense. At the age of twenty-one, she killed a Nazi colonel with her pistol.

Virginia Hall, called the Limping Lady, receives the Distinguished Service Cross in 1945. She was the first nonmilitary woman to receive the award.

The Limping Lady was Virginia Hall. She was born to a wealthy family in Baltimore, Maryland, in 1906. She limped because she had lost her leg in a hunting accident. She walked with a wooden leg that she called Cuthbert. In 1940 Hall was living in France. Not long after, she made her way to England. Hall joined the newly formed spy agency Office of Strategic Services (OSS).

Hall found areas where planes could drop supplies using parachutes for the Resistance.

Then she returned to France where she secretly helped train three Resistance **battalions** to wage guerrilla warfare against the Nazis. Hall worked behind enemy lines to map drop zones where Allies could leave weapons for Resistance fighters. She set up safe houses where members of the Resistance could hide from the Nazis. And she provided a steady stream of information to the Allies about Nazi troop movements and battle plans.

After the war ended, Hall did not talk much about her wartime activities. But her actions saved many lives. In 1943 King George VI presented her with the Order of the British Empire medal for her service. And in 1945, she received the Distinguished Cross for her bravery. In 2006, long after her death, she was honored again. French president Jacques Chirac said, "Virginia Hall is a true hero of the French Resistance."

CHAPTER 4
A SPY BEHIND HOME PLATE

In 1934, before the start of the war, an American all-star baseball team traveled to Tokyo, Japan. The team was there to play a series of friendly games against the Japanese all-star team. Two of baseball's greatest players, Babe Ruth and Lou Gehrig, were on the

Left to right: Jimmie Foxx, Babe Ruth, and Lou Gehrig were three of the American all-stars playing baseball in Japan in 1934.

A view of a naval base near Tokyo
during an air raid in 1942

American team. Morris (Moe) Berg also played. Berg
was a third-string catcher with a poor batting average.
Many of the American players wondered why Berg was
on the team at all. But while he was there, he snuck
onto the roof of Tokyo's tallest building. He brought a
movie camera with him and filmed the city's harbor
and factories. Berg later showed his videos to the
American military. In 1942 the United States bombed
Tokyo. Many believe the military used Berg's videos to
plan the raid.

Moe Berg in 1933

A CHILDHOOD HOBBY

As a boy, Berg had had two hobbies: baseball and learning foreign languages. By the time Berg graduated from college in 1923, he knew seven languages, including Japanese, German, and French. Berg went on to play baseball for the Chicago White Sox, the Cleveland Indians, and other major-league teams for fifteen seasons.

In 1943 the OSS recruited Berg. The OSS feared that the Nazis were working to develop an atom bomb. Scientists Albert Einstein and Leo Szilard had first warned the US government in 1939 about Nazi efforts to build an atom bomb. If the Nazis were to complete such a bomb, they might win the war.

Berg traveled to Germany in 1944 and spoke with the German atomic scientist Werner Heisenberg. Berg

Werner Heisenberg won the 1932 Nobel Prize in Physics. During World War II, he worked on nuclear research for Germany.

had been ordered to kill Heisenberg if he thought the scientist had learned how to build an atom bomb. But Berg determined that Heisenberg had not yet figured out the complex science needed to create an atom bomb. Berg returned to the United States without harming Heisenberg.

A WINNING EFFORT

Berg and the other secret agents and spies of World War II did not fight on the battlefield. Instead, they

STEM HIGHLIGHT

Throughout World War II, the United States and Germany raced to build an atom bomb. Atomic weapons get their power through a nuclear reaction called fission, which splits an atom into smaller parts, releasing a huge amount of energy. In August 1945, the United States dropped two atom bombs on Japanese cities Nagasaki (*right*) and Hiroshima. The bombs caused devastating destruction. World War II ended soon after these attacks.

worked behind the scenes to disrupt Axis war efforts. Information gathered by spies helped the Allies plan bombing raids and ground attacks. Secret agents stopped the Axis powers from building secret weapons. And they helped members of the Resistance fight back against the Nazis. Each individual effort was small, but together the work of the spies and secret agents helped the Allies defeat the Axis powers. The war in Europe ended when Nazi Germany surrendered on May 7, 1945. And a few months later, on September 2, Japan surrendered to the Allies. World War II was over.

1925	American singer and dancer Josephine Baker moves to Paris.
1934	Pro baseball player and spy Morris (Moe) Berg secretly films the Tokyo skyline while visiting Japan for an all-star game.
September 1, 1939	World War II begins in Europe when Nazi Germany invades Poland.
June 1940	Nazi Germany conquers France.
1942	British Naval Intelligence officer Ian Fleming forms a top-secret group called 30 AU.
June 6, 1944	The Allied invasion of France, known as D-day, begins.
May 7, 1945	World War II ends in Europe when the Allies defeat Nazi Germany.

August 1945	The United States drops atom bombs on Hiroshima and Nagasaki, Japan.
September 2, 1945	World War II ends.
1948	Novelist Graham Greene publishes the best-selling novel *The Heart of the Matter*, based on his spy activities during World War II.
1953	Ian Fleming publishes the first James Bond spy novel, based on his experiences in World War II.

SOURCE NOTES

10 Clarence Lusane, *Hitler's Black Victims* (New York: Routledge, 2003), 218.

16 Patrick K. O'Donnell, *Operatives, Spies, and Saboteurs: The Unknown Story of the Men and Women of World War II's OSS* (New York: Free Press, 2004), 173.

21 Cate Lineberry, "WANTED: The Limping Lady," *Smithsonian.com*, February 1, 2007, http://www.smithsonianmag.com/history /wanted-the-limping-lady-146541513.

GLOSSARY

barges: flat-bottomed boats used to carry freight

battalions: large bodies of troops ready for battle

commandos: units of troops trained to make surprise raids in enemy territory

disguise: an altered appearance meant to hide one's identity

explosives: substances that can be used to blow something up

guerrilla warfare: military activities such as ambushes and sabotage conducted by small groups of irregular soldiers against larger forces

Nazis: German soldiers in World War II. *Nazi* was also the name of a political party led by Adolf Hitler that took over Germany in 1933 and invaded many European countries.

vapor: a substance in the form of a gas

FURTHER INFORMATION

Bearce, Stephanie. *Spies, Secret Missions, and Hidden Facts from World War II*. Waco, TX: Prufock, 2015.

Crafty Gadgets and Famous Spies of WWII
https://www.warhistoryonline.com/war-articles/crafty-gadgets
-tricks-famous-wwii-spies.html

Doeden, Matt. *World War II Resistance Fighters*. Minneapolis: Lerner Publications, 2018.

Landau, Elaine. *Assassins, Traitors, and Spies*. Minneapolis: Lerner Publications, 2013.

Mitchell, Susan K. *Spy Gizmos and Gadgets*. Berkeley Heights, NJ: Enslow, 2012.

Secrets, Lies, and Atomic Spies: 20th-Century Deceptions
http://www.pbs.org/wgbh/nova/venona/deceptions.html

World War II
https://www.cia.gov/kids-page/6-12th-grade/operation-history
/world-war-ii.html

World War II: Spies and Secret Agents
http://www.ducksters.com/history/world_war_ii/spies_and_
secret_agents_of_ww2.php

Index

Photo Acknowledgments

The images in this book are used with the permission of: design: © iStockphoto.com/akinshin (barbed wire); © iStockphoto.com/ElementalImaging (camouflage background); © iStockphoto.com/aaron007 (barbed wire frame); Sueddeutsche Zeitung Photo/Alamy Stock Photo, pp. 4–5; National Portrait Gallery, London, p. 6; © Laura Westlund/Independent Picture Service, p. 7; © Popperfoto/Getty Images, p. 8; Everett Collection Inc/Alamy Stock Photo, p. 9; © Gamma-Keystone/Getty Images, p. 10; © Jacques Boyer/Roger-Viollet /The Image Works, p. 11 (top); © Jacques Boye/Roger-Viollet/The Image Works, p. 11 (bottom); © Express/Express/Getty Images, p. 12; Pictorial Press Ltd/Alamy Stock Photo, p. 13; © Kurt Hutton/Getty Images, p. 14; Photo 12/Alamy Stock Photo, p. 15; Pictorial Press Ltd/Alamy Stock Photo, p. 16; Chronicle/Alamy Stock Photo, p. 17; National Archives (595150), p. 19; AP Photo, p. 20; National Baseball Hall of Fame Library, Cooperstown, N.Y., p. 22; © Corbis/Getty Images, p. 23; © Stanley Weston/Getty Images, p. 24; The Granger Collection, New York, p. 25; Ian Dagnall/Alamy Stock Photo, p. 26.

Cover: © CORBIS/Getty Images.